Learning Centers for
Confirmation

LEARNING CENTERS *for* Confirmation

Doris Murphy

TWENTY THIRD 23rd
PUBLICATIONS

TWENTY-THIRD PUBLICATIONS
A Division of Bayard
One Montauk Avenue, Suite 200
New London, CT 06320
(860) 437-3012 or (800) 321-0411
www.23rdpublications.com

ISBN 978-1-58595-757-6

Library of Congress Catalog Card Number: 2009903441
Printed in the U.S.A.

Table of Contents

Learning Centers for
Confirmation

Introduction

In the restored Rite of Christian Initiation, the sacrament of confirmation is celebrated with baptism and Eucharist. In this rite, confirmation is a sacrament of initiation into the Christian community. Confirmation outside of this context is more difficult to teach and explain and more difficult for recipients to fully understand.

In many parishes today, however, confirmation is celebrated in high school. Many catechists see this as an opportunity to teach the candidates every church doctrine as if they will never again study about their faith. Or, a program may consist of hours of service projects, as if the candidates had not been actively living the gospel up to this time. The *confirmandi* are told they will receive the Holy Spirit, as if what took place with the coming of the Spirit at their baptism was insignificant.

So then, is confirmation about doctrine? Is it about service, about adult commitment? Or is it about initiation—a beginning—or about completion—an ending—not unlike graduation?

In a way it is all these things, and so these learning centers provide an opportunity for teenagers to acknowledge the Holy Spirit already active in their lives and invite them to better understand the sacraments that initiate them into the Christian community. They focus on baptism, the Eucharist, the Mass, the Holy Spirit, the works of mercy, Catholic social teaching, and much more.

Learning centers are one means for helping parents and other adults get involved in the religious formation of children in non-intimidating and practical ways. Many parents are eager to learn more about their own faith and want to hand that faith on to their children, but they don't feel they have adequate training or enough information to do so. Yet parents share their faith best through example, family rituals, and conversations. Learning centers can help them extend this process. This practical method of faith sharing can be used with almost any doctrinal content when presented in an age-appropriate manner with sensitivity to various learning styles.

Here parents are provided the opportunity to complete hands-on tasks, have discussions/conversations about their faith with their children, and reinforce material that is addressed in their children's textbooks.

Learning centers offer creative and interactive ways to do this. Plus they are flexible. Parents can choose a convenient time to visit the center with their children and work at their own pace. It usually takes about two hours to thoughtfully visit the sessions and complete the activities. Learning centers also give the director of faith formation an opportunity to observe parents, children, and other adults working together. This can help him or her determine which learning centers are most beneficial in the learning process.

Special thanks to Carol Mercord, Religious Education Director at St. Joseph Parish, Prescott, Wisconsin, for her continued encouragement and suggestions. Also to Tessa Schuermann, Youth Minister at St. Bridget's Parish in River Falls, Wisconsin, for sharing her ideas and expertise.

Letter to Parents

Dear Parents,

Thank you so much for your participation in these confirmation learning centers. We hope this will be a good opportunity for you and your son or daughter to talk, to share, to pray, and to grow in faith together. We hope it will also be a good opportunity for you to renew your own commitment to your Catholic faith. Please take time to consider the following questions—either before you visit the centers or afterward when you have more time for reflection.

- How do you feel about your own faith at this point in your life? Are you struggling? Growing? Strong? Weak? Is how you live your faith even an issue for you at this time?

- Can you remember when you were the age of your child? What similarities or differences are there between then and now in terms of the faith/religion/church situation? Were there things happening in your life at that time that your child does not have to deal with now? Vice versa?

- How do you think you are handing on your Catholic faith to your child? How do you measure your success or failure?

- Can you think of any recent situations when you talked to your child one on one about his or her faith and relationship with God? What happened?

- How are you personally involved in regular weekend worship? Does your child regularly attend Mass? What happens when he or she objects to attending?

- Does your son or daughter attend religion classes but not Mass? Why has this happened?

- What help do you expect from your parish with the continuing development of your child's faith? What are your expectations for his or her confirmation preparation?

May God bless you for all you have done as a parent. You have graciously and faithfully brought your son or daughter to the table of the Lord, and now you are walking with him or her as he or she prepares to celebrate confirmation, an important step in their lifelong journey of faith.

Group Gathering
Prayers

Parents, sponsors, and candidates may gather with a parish leader for prayer before and after participating in these centers with a parish leader. There is an Opening Gathering Prayer and a Closing Gathering Prayer.

All In the name of the Father and of the Son and of the Holy Spirit. Amen.
We come before you, Spirit of God.
Come to us, remain with us, and enlighten our hearts.
Give us light and strength to know your will,
to make it our own, and to live it in our lives.
Guide us by your wisdom, support us by your power,
for you are God, sharing the glory of Father and Son.
You desire justice for all.
Enable us to uphold the rights of others.
Unite us to yourself and keep us faithful to all that is true.
As we gather in your name, we pray that all our decisions
may be pleasing to you
and that we may be good and faithful servants.
You live and reign with the Father and the Son,
one God, forever and ever.

Candidate(s) Amen.

Parent/Sponsor Come, Holy Spirit, fill the hearts of your faithful.

Candidate(s) And kindle in them the fire of your love.

Parent/Sponsor Send forth your Spirit and they shall be created.

All And you will renew the face of the earth.

Parent/Sponsor Let us pray.
Lord by the light of the Holy Spirit you have taught the hearts of your faithful.
In the same Spirit, help us to relish what is right and always rejoice in your love.
We ask this through Christ our Lord.

All Amen.

All	"We Are Called" (song)
Parent/Sponsor	Acts of the Apostles 8:14–22, 25
Candidate(s)	With the support of our families, our sponsors, and this parish, we choose to commit ourselves completely to preparing for the sacrament of confirmation. We understand that by committing ourselves to this process, we will try to learn more about our faith, to serve others willingly, to reflect on and deepen our relationship with God, Jesus, and the Holy Spirit, and to become witnesses of the gospel.
All	"Here I Am, Lord" (song)
Parent/Sponsor	*(lay hands on the shoulders of the candidates and pray silently for a few moments)*
All	The Apostles' Creed I believe in God, the Father Almighty, Creator of heaven and earth; and in Jesus Christ, his only Son, our Lord; who was conceived by the Holy Spirit, born of the Virgin Mary, suffered under Pontius Pilate, was crucified, died, and was buried. He descended into hell; the third day he rose again from the dead; he ascended into heaven, and is seated at the right hand of God, the Father Almighty; from thence he shall come to judge the living and the dead. I believe in the Holy Spirit, the holy Catholic Church, the communion of saints, the forgiveness of sins, the resurrection of the body, and life everlasting. Amen.

Now offer one another a sign of peace.

Learning Centers for
Confirmation

At each center prepare the following:

- *A plastic page holder or laminated copy of the guidelines for the center. You will find the information for these at the beginning of each section: title, church teaching, goal, Bible verse, what you will learn, directions, and background*
- *Worksheets as needed for each participant*
- *A Bible (with a marker at the appropriate passage)*
- *Supplies as indicated for completing each project*

Note: *The letter for the parents with the list of learning centers should be available at the registration table for each participant.*

Your Christian Life Begins

Goal

To understand that the Christian life begins with the sacraments of initiation: baptism, confirmation, and Eucharist

Church Teaching

Catechism of the Catholic Church, paragraph 1212

The sacraments of initiation—baptism, confirmation, and the Eucharist—lay the *foundations* of every Christian life….By means of these sacraments of Christian initiation, [the faithful] thus receive in increasing measure the divine life and advance toward the perfection of charity.

Bible Verse

Romans 6:3–5

What You Will Learn

That sacraments are the foundation of the Catholic-Christian life
The history of initiation and the RCIA process
Sacraments are a "beginning," not an end on your journey of faith

Supplies

Bible
Direction sheet
Worksheet "Stages of Faith"
Prayer activity
Dish of water

Directions for the Center

- Read Romans 6:3–5.

- Read the information and directions provided at the center.

- Talk about your own baptism, confirmation, and first Eucharist with your son or daughter—especially if you celebrated these when you were older.

- Ask your son or daughter what he/she recalls being told about his/her baptism or First Communion. What do you remember about these celebrations?

- Follow the directions for the worksheet "Stages of Faith."

- Share the short prayer activity.

Background

In contemporary parish practice, children are usually baptized when they are infants, receive their First Communion at about age seven, and are generally confirmed as teenagers.

In the early Christian Church people received all three of these sacraments as adults after going through a process of preparation. This process, known today as RCIA (Rite of Christian Initiation of Adults), was restored to full use after Vatican Council II (1963–1965). Today, adults who want to be initiated into the Catholic Church spend about a year preparing. This preparation period culminates at the Easter Vigil in the celebration of the sacraments of baptism, confirmation, and Eucharist.

Stages of Faith

People grow in their faith just as they grow in other aspects of their lives. This growth in faith generally occurs in stages (simplified here into four stages for your discussion). *Read about these stages and then follow the directions.*

STAGE ONE: IMITATING
(pre-school and primary grades)

At this stage children learn from those around them, primarily parents and extended family or adult caregivers. They learn to imitate prayer, attendance at Mass, doing good deeds, etc.

STAGE THREE: SEARCHING
(high school and college)

It is very important at this stage to ask questions about the faith, the church, and about God. Parents and other adults need to be present as guides on this search, encouraging healthy questions even concerning other religions.

STAGE TWO: AFFILIATING
(middle and junior high school)

Children at this stage want to be involved in church, school, home, and community activities. They want to join teams and clubs. They want to be part of church activities. At home they like to participate in meal prayer, rituals, and family religious traditions.

STAGE FOUR: OWNING
(young adulthood and beyond)

This is the time when adults recognize that they do not have all the answers and that there will be ups and downs in one's faith journey. However, they choose the Catholic Church as home for themselves. The prayers and rituals, especially the sacraments, continue to lead them to holiness as they cooperate with the grace (life in the Spirit) that God offers. They understand that learning about their faith is a lifetime commitment.

CANDIDATES: Discuss/share your experiences of stages one and two.

PARENTS: Discuss/share your experiences of stages three and four.

TOGETHER: Discuss/share where you are right now (especially the candidates)

Parent   (*with the holy water, make the Sign of the Cross on your child's forehead while saying this prayer*)
Dear God, help us to grow in faith each day and open our hearts to your Spirit.

Child   We ask this in Jesus' name. Amen.

You are Called at Baptism

Goal

To understand how at baptism each of us is called by name to become an active member of the Christian community

Church Teaching

Catechism of the Catholic Church, paragraph 1213

Through baptism we are freed from sin and reborn as sons of God; we become members of Christ, are incorporated into the Church, and made sharers in her mission....

Bible Verse

1 Samuel 3:2–18

What You Will Learn

God calls you by name. The rite of baptism (of children) says: "What name do you give your child?" The rite of confirmation says: "If possible, each candidate is called by name..."

At baptism you join the communion of saints, the living and dead. As an infant, you may have been given the name of one of the saints to guide you on your journey of faith

Supplies

Bible
Direction sheet
Worksheet "Saints: Then and Now"
Pencils

Directions for the Center

- Read 1 Samuel 3:2–18.

- Read the information and directions provided at the center.

- Together read the names of the saints and share their brief biographies.

- Talk about people you may know or have heard about whose lives are/were much like the lives of one of these saints. Why do you think it's important to have "heroes/heroines" who are saintly (holy)?

Background

When initiated into the Christian community, the early Christians were given a new or additional name as they took on a new identity in Christ. They were called by name into God's family. Since baptism and confirmation were part of the same celebration, the name was the same. Today candidates are older and may want to choose an additional saint name to signify their deeper awareness of what it means to be a disciple of Christ.

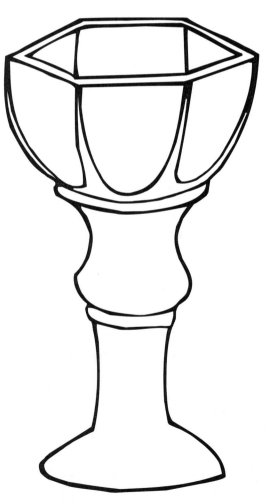

Adding names is common in some cultures. When a Hmong man becomes a father, a "mature name" ceremony is held to give him a new name indicating that he has passed from one stage of life to another stage entailing more responsibility. His given name may be "Sao," his clan name "Thao," and his mature name could be "Chu Sao Thao." In a similar manner, Native Americans often add a new name expressing an important life-changing event in their lives, for example, Running Bear, Black Elk, Flowering Rose.

If a confirmation candidate adds a name it should be a saint or biblical character who would be a guide on their faith journey and a role model for their lives.

Saints: Then and Now

Read these brief biographies and then write the name of someone you may know who reminds you of this saint.

SAINTS AND SAINTLY PERSONS	BRIEF BIOGRAPHY	*Who is like this saint today?*
Peter, apostle	The leader of the early church; first bishop of Rome; professed his faith saying, "You are the Christ, the Son of the Living God"	
Mary Magdalene	Called the apostle to the apostles; one of the faithful women who followed Jesus with his disciples; the first to discover the empty tomb after the death of Jesus	
Thomas Aquinas	Perhaps the most famous theologian and doctor of the church; wrote the *Summa Theologica* in the thirteenth century, a systematic study of the Christian faith	
Catherine of Siena	A fourteenth-century mystic; was a peacemaker among factions in the church; a doctor-scholar of the church	
Dorothy Day	Co-founded the Catholic Worker Movement in 1933, working directly with the poor and for peace; known for her works of charity and justice; died in 1980	
Archbishop Oscar Romero	Became "a voice for the voiceless poor" in Central America; martyred in 1980 in San Salvador while celebrating Mass	
Mother Teresa of Calcutta	Founded the Missionaries of Charity in India; her sisters are now in every urban city in the world serving those who suffer from poverty of spirit as much as material poverty	
Thérèse of Lisieux	Known as the Little Flower; lived her short life in solitude in a Carmelite monastery; her holiness became known through her writings after her death; called her spirituality "the Little Way"	
Maximilian Kolbe	A concentration camp martyr who gave his life to save another prisoner; devoted to Mary, the Mother of Jesus	

SAINTS AND SAINTLY PERSONS	BRIEF BIOGRAPHY	Who is like this saint today?
Francis of Assisi	Started a community of brothers who lived a simple life of poverty; saw God's presence in all of creation; his followers today are called Franciscans	
Hildegarde of Bingen	Artist, poet, musician, author, and theologian; headed a large Benedictine monastery of women in the twelfth century; her writings on ecology and spirituality are still relevant today	
Cardinal John Henry Newman	Scholar who converted from the Anglican Church to Roman Catholic; co-founded the Oxford movement (scholars in dialogue about religious tradition and the modern world) in the nineteenth century; confronted church leaders when truth was being compromised	
Thomas More	Successful lawyer and chancellor to the king of England; opposed the king's decision to become head of the church in England; beheaded for taking this stand against political authority	
Agnes	One of the first saint-martyrs in the early church who chose death rather than deny her Christianity	
Paul	Spread the news of the gospel through many journeys; his letters to various communities became the foundational documents for the early church	
Nicholas	Patron of children, protector of those whose lives are threatened by poverty, violence, or exploitation; on his feast, gifts are delivered to deserving children	
Rose Hawthorne	Daughter of Nathaniel Hawthorne; started homes for those with incurable cancer in the late 1800s; though not attributed to her, her ideas started the hospice movement	

If you will be choosing an additional saint's name (someone living or deceased), what will it be? _____

Why? _____

_____

You Are Gospel People

Goal

To understand that Christians are recognized by their faithfulness to the gospel

Church Teaching

Catechism of the Catholic Church, paragraphs 1696, 1309

Preparation for confirmation should aim at leading the Christian toward a more intimate union with Christ and a more lively familiarity with the Holy Spirit—his actions, his gifts, and his biddings—in order to be more capable of assuming the apostolic responsibilities of Christian life. (#1309)

Bible Verses

Matthew 11:29
Matthew 5
John 14:6

What You Will Learn

To distinguish behaviors and attitudes common to Christians
To let others guide us by their advice and care to be better Christians
How the Beatitudes direct the way of life for us as Christians

Supplies

Bible
Direction sheet
Worksheet "Qualities of a Christian"
Pencils

Directions for Center

- Read Matthew 11:29; Matthew 5; John 14:6.

- Read the information and directions provided at the center.

- Follow the directions on the worksheet.

Background

Christians are called at baptism to be children of God, made in the image of God. We are called to imitate Jesus who is the way, the truth, and the life. The Beatitudes (Matthew 5) are the ultimate guide for us on our journey.

Qualities of a Christian

Read through the list of words on this sheet.
 a. Underline those characteristics that you already see in yourself.
 b. Circle those characteristics that you would like to see in yourself.
 c. Discuss with your parent/sponsor which words they think best describe you at the present.
 d. Which three qualities in particular do you want to continue to develop as a Christian?

cooperative	helpful	diligent
confident	sincere	honest
considerate	creative	decisive
serious	aggressive	open-minded
compulsive	stubborn	personable
ambitious	persistent	loving
gregarious	peacemaker	friendly
responsible	competitive	self-controlled
anxious	assertive	forgiving
hopeful	trusting	dreamer
courageous	daring	tolerant
compassionate	merciful	caring
unique	consistent	obedient
amusing	fair	concerned
kind	patient	dependable
gentle	warm	interdependent
independent	passive	grateful
idealistic	understanding	just
brave	joyful	humble
responsible	thoughtful	

You Are Anointed

Goal

To deepen the belief that at confirmation you are anointed as priest, king, and prophet

Church Teaching

Catechism of the Catholic Church, paragraphs 1546, 1293, 783–785

Anointing, in biblical and other ancient symbolism, is rich in meaning: oil is a sign of abundance and joy; it cleanses (anointing before and after a bath) and limbers (the anointing of athletes and wrestlers); oil is a sign of healing, since it is soothing to bruises and wounds; and it makes radiant with beauty, health, and strength. (#1293)

Jesus Christ is the one whom the Father anointed with the Holy Spirit and established as priest, prophet, and king. The whole people of God participates in these three offices of Christ and bears the responsibilities for mission and service that flow from them. (#783)

Bible Verse

1 Peter 4:10

What You Will Learn

How you can serve the church community as priest, prophet, and king
Ministry means involvement in church worship as well as service to others
Oil is an important symbol for confirmation

Supplies

Bible
Direction sheet
Worksheet "Priest, Prophet, King"
Pencils
Dish of oil (baby or body oil)

Directions for Center

- Read 1 Peter 4:10.

- Read the information and directions.

- When we are anointed at baptism/confirmation we are designated as priest (prayer), prophet (teacher and do-er of justice), and king (leader). Discuss how you can express each of these in your service to others. Use the worksheet and match your service to each category. Can you think of some other ways you can serve the church and others?

- When you have completed the sheet, ask your parent/sponsor to anoint your hands with the oil saying, "Soon you will be sealed with the gift of the Holy Spirit." You answer, "Amen."

Background

Rituals in the church are meant to emphasize the presence of the Spirit. The anointing with oil is a sign of strength, soothing, abundance, blessing, healing, and consecration. Kings, prophets, and priests were anointed in the Old Testament. This signified to the people that those anointed were chosen by God and had a special role of service. It is God's desire to bless us, and oil is a symbol of this blessing.

Priest, Prophet, King

Titles can be empty promises or they can direct us to live very meaningful lives as we minister in the church and the world. *Put the correct number (1, 2, or 3) before the appropriate acts of service below.*

1
PRIEST
(worship and prayer)

2
PROPHET
(teacher and do-er of justice)

3
KING
(servant leader)

____ church decorating

____ eucharistic minister

____ work at the food pantry

____ give good advice to a friend

____ use my talents and gifts

____ help my neighbors

____ forgive someone

____ usher

____ lead by example

____ visit a care center

____ rake leaves for someone

____ serve at liturgy

____ join the church choir

____ be a class leader

____ help at a homeless shelter

____ join a peace march

____ contribute to a charity organization

____ show kindness to the "underdog"

____ spend time before the Blessed Sacrament in prayer

____ shovel snow for the elderly

____ don't demand first place

____ give clothes to Good Will

____ lead family prayer at home

____ assist a catechist in religion class

I am priestly when I...

I am prophetic when I...

I am kingly when I...

You Are God's Chosen One

Goal

To understand that on your lifelong faith journey, God speaks to your heart through Scripture saying: "I will be your God and you will be my people"

Church Teaching

Catechism of the Catholic Church, paragraph 1102

The proclamation [of faith] does not stop with a teaching; it elicits the *response of faith* as consent and commitment, directed at the covenant between God and his people. Once again it is the Holy Spirit who gives the grace of faith, strengthens it, and makes it grow in the community.

Bible Verse

Jeremiah 31:31–34

What You Will Learn

In biblical terms, a covenant is different from a contract. A contract is a legal agreement with another. A covenant is a profound relationship with God, as in baptism, or with another person as in marriage

To reflect on our lifelong journey as it influences our faith

Supplies

Bible
Direction sheet
Worksheet "Your Life Journey"
Pencils

Directions for Center

- Read Jeremiah 31:31–34.

- Read the information and directions.

- Use the worksheet for discussing your life journey with your parent/sponsor. Your life journey and your growth in faith influence one another.

Background

A covenant is a solemn agreement between human beings or between human beings and God. It involves mutual commitments. In the Old Testament, God made covenants with Noah, Abraham, and Moses. In the New Testament, Christ gave us a new and eternal covenant, the Eucharist, sealed by his death and resurrection. Each of us makes a personal covenant with God at baptism. Our "covenant-agreement" comes from the heart; it is not just a legal document. We do not take our part of the covenant lightly after we are confirmed. We truly believe and identify the words: "God will be our God and we will be God's people."

Your Life Journey

Throughout your life journey, you have opportunities to honor your covenant with God: through the people you meet, the events in your life, as well as through your failures and accomplishments. All have a direct influence on your relationship with God.

PEOPLE *(List the names of two or three people who are or have been very important to you up to this point in your life. Why are these people important to you?)*

FUTURE DREAMS/GOALS *(List one or two goals you have for your future and how you hope to attain these goals.)*

IMPORTANT EVENTS *(Describe one or two events that have made a lasting impression on you.)*

OBSTACLES *(Describe one failure or disappointment you have experienced so far in your life.)*

ACCOMPLISHMENTS *(Describe one or two accomplishments that you are especially proud of achieving.)*

You Are Nourished by the Eucharist

Goal

To deepen your understanding that the Eucharist is the source and summit of your faith

Church Teaching

Catechism of the Catholic Church, paragraph 1374

> The mode of Christ's presence under the eucharistic species is unique....This presence is called "real"...because it is presence in the fullest sense: that is to say, it is a *substantial* presence by which Christ, God and man, makes himself wholly and entirely present.

Bible Verse

1 Corinthians 11:23–27

What You Will Learn

To renew your belief and commitment in the continuing presence of Jesus in the Eucharist

To study various words that tell you more about the Eucharist

To acknowledge the various ways you can recognize the presence of Jesus in your midst

Supplies

Bible
Direction sheet
Loaf of bread (freshly made, if possible) and song words
Worksheet "Learning about Eucharist"
Pencils
Answers (if needed): *11; 7; 1; 2; 13; 14; 3; 9; 4; 12; 8; 5; 10; 6*

Directions for Center

- Read 1 Corinthians 11:23–27.

- Read the information and directions.

- Pray the closing prayer together.

Background

At the Eucharist we are fed as a community with Jesus, the Bread of Life. Since the Eucharist is so central to our religious faith celebrations, it is important to deepen our understanding of it. We celebrate the continuing presence of Jesus in our midst. We believe Christ is truly present in the Eucharist. The Vatican II *Constitution on the Liturgy* tells us that "Christ is truly present in the word, in the presider, in the gathered assembly, and especially in the Eucharist" (#7).

Here are four key terms:

assembly: all of us gathered at the Eucharist. We are the body of Christ, called to live and act as followers of Christ

the word: the Scripture readings from the book called the Lectionary

presider: the priest-leader who calls us to be a "holy people" through actions and the prayers of the Mass, contained in the Sacramentary

Eucharist: the continuing true presence of Jesus in the form of bread and wine

Learning about Eucharist

Many words are used in explaining the Eucharist. Often these originated in the early church and had special meaning during that time. Do you know what they mean for us now? *Try to match the words and definitions below.*

NOTE: Some of these terms are very difficult to define. If you can't match them, you might want to take this page home and look for information on the Internet.

WORDS

____ Transubstantiation

____ Anamnesis

____ Epiclesis

____ "in persona Christi"

____ Memorial acclamation

____ Presence of Christ

____ Ministers of the altar

____ Body of Christ

____ Genuflection

____ Altar

____ Presider's chair

____ Sacrifice

____ Lectern

____ Tabernacle

DEFINITIONS

1. the priest asks God to send the Holy Spirit so the bread and wine become the Body and Blood of Jesus *(Hint: It begins with an "e")*

2. anointed at Holy Orders, the priest celebrating the Eucharist acts in the name of Jesus *(Hint: It's a Latin term)*

3. those who use their gifts in service at the celebration of the Eucharist (servers, lectors, eucharistic, for example)

4. a reverent gesture as we enter the pew to express adoration of the Blessed Sacrament

5. offering made to God on behalf of the people; in this way Christ's death on the cross is remembered anew

6. the receptacle where the Eucharist is reserved for communion for the sick and other uses

7. the "remembrance" of God's saving deeds; calls to mind the passion, death, and resurrection of Jesus *(Hint: Begins with an "a")*

8. where the presider sits and calls the community to prayer

9. the church is given this name because of the intimate union of Jesus and the community

10. it is from here that the readings are proclaimed

11. describes the unique change of the eucharistic bread and wine into the Body and Blood of Christ *(Hint: It begins with a "t")*

12. the center and focal point of the church where Christ is made present under sacramental signs in the Mass

13. the moment at Mass when we proclaim the mystery of our faith: Christ has died, Christ has risen, Christ will come again

14. Jesus continues to be truly among us at each Eucharist, wholly and entirely, in the fullest sense

Closing Prayer

Gracious God, it is with great joy that
   we gather as believers to give you
      praise and thanks.
We believe Christ is present
   in the gathered community,
   in the Word of God that is proclaimed,
   in the presider who calls us to
      prayer and to holiness,
   and, especially, as we come to your table and recognize
      your continuing presence,
         when we eat your body and drink your blood.
Help us be grateful for this gracious gift.
We pray this in Jesus' name.
Amen.

*Now share a piece of the bread and, after eating
it, pray the Our Father together.*

You Give Thanks and Remember

Goal

To understand more fully that we come together as a community to express thanks to God and to remember what God has done and continues to do for us.

The "Amen" we say means "Yes, I believe"

Church Teaching

Catechism of the Catholic Church, paragraph 1408

The eucharistic celebration always includes the proclamation of the word of God; thanksgiving to God the Father for all his benefits, above all the gifts of his Son; the consecration of the bread and wine; and participation in the liturgical banquet by receiving the Lord's body and blood. These elements constitute one single act of worship.

What You Will Learn

To review the order of the Mass

To recall the meaning of each part of the eucharistic celebration

The word Mass—*missa*—means to be sent out to live the word and the Eucharist, which we have celebrated together

To understand that we gather together to proclaim our faith that Christ has died, is risen, and will come again. This is the mystery of our faith lived out at this Eucharist and in our daily lives

Supplies

Bible

Direction sheet

Envelopes containing words and definitions for parts of the Mass (cut apart)

Copy of the Creed as a "holy card" or bookmark

Answers (if needed): Opening Hymn; Penitential Rite; Gloria; Opening Prayer; First Reading; Psalm Response; Second Reading; Gospel Acclamation; Gospel; Homily; Creed; General Intercessions; Presentation/Preparation of Gifts; Prayer over Gifts; Preface; Holy, Holy; Consecration; Memorial Acclamation; Lord's Prayer; Sign of Peace; Lamb of God; Communion; Prayer after Communion; Blessing and Dismissal

Directions for Center

- Read the directions.

- Discuss with your sponsor/parent some of the important events in your life or the lives of your ancestors that you want to remember. Why is it important to do this? The Creed (to believe) tells us what we come to Mass to remember. The words of remembering in the Eucharistic prayer (anamnesis) bring the past, present, and future together for us.

- Take an envelope containing the parts of the Mass and put them into the correct order.

- Take a copy of the Apostles' Creed home with you. Pray this each evening from now until your confirmation and reflect on the mysteries we believe as Christians.

Order of the Mass

Cut these apart and place them in an envelope.

PENITENTIAL RITE We recall our sins and the need for mercy and reconciliation	**HOMILY** The presider shares reflections on the message of God's word which we have just heard	**CONSECRATION** The words that recall Christ's actions at the Last Supper; through these words and power of the Spirit (epiclesis) Jesus again becomes present in the bread and wine
BLESSING AND DISMISSAL We are sent forth to live the Eucharist with strength and courage	**PROFESSION OF FAITH (CREED)** We stand to profess what we believe	**GLORIA** We sing this joyful hymn of praise
PRESENTATION AND PREPARATION OF GIFTS We bring our gifts of bread and wine to the altar; we also offer ourselves	**MEMORIAL ACCLAMATION** We proclaim our belief in Jesus' death, resurrection, and final coming	**SIGN OF PEACE** The community shares a sign of peace to show we forgive and love one another

SECOND READING We listen to a reading from the letters of the New Testament	**OPENING PRAYER** The presider gathers together all our needs and presents them to God; we respond, "Amen"	**PRAYER OVER GIFTS** The presider invites us to pray with him that God will accept our gifts
LORD'S PRAYER As we prepare to receive communion, we pray the prayer that Jesus taught us	**FIRST READING** The lector proclaims a reading from the Old Testament; we answer, "Thanks be to God"	**COMMUNION** We receive Jesus in the bread and wine and say "Amen," which means "Yes, I believe"
PSALM RESPONSE We respond to God's word in the reading through the words and music of a psalm	**PREFACE; EUCHARISTIC PRAYER** The presider begins this great prayer by praising God for the wonderful works of creation and redemption	**LAMB OF GOD** We sing this litany for the breaking of the bread, asking for mercy and peace

GOSPEL We stand as we listen to the good news proclaimed; we respond, "Praise to you, Lord Jesus Christ"	**OPENING HYMN** We begin our celebration together by praising God through song and joining as one united community	**HOLY, HOLY; AMEN** At the end of the preface we join all creation in praise to the Father through Jesus; at the end of the Eucharistic Prayer we sing, "Amen"
GOSPEL ACCLAMATION We prepare to hear the good news by standing and singing "Alleluia"	**PRAYER AFTER COMMUNION** The presider prays that our reception of Jesus will change us—that we will be more like Jesus	**GENERAL INTERCESSIONS** We pray for those who are in need

THE APOSTLES' CREED

I believe in God, the Father Almighty.
creator of heaven and earth.

I believe in Jesus Christ,
his only Son, our Lord.
He was conceived
by the power of the Holy Spirit
and born of the Virgin Mary.
He suffered under Pontius Pilate,
was crucified, died, and was buried.
He descended to the dead.
On the third day he rose again.
He ascended into heaven,
and is seated at the right hand of the Father.
He will come again
to judge the living and the dead.

I believe in the Holy Spirit,
the holy Catholic Church,
the communion of saints,
the forgiveness of sins,
the resurrection of the body,
and the life everlasting. Amen.

You Receive Special Gifts

Goal

To learn how the gifts of the Spirit bring an awareness of how we can live as "God-filled people"

Church Teaching

Catechism of the Catholic Church, paragraphs 1830–1831

The moral life of Christians is sustained by the gifts of the Holy Spirit. (#1830)

The seven *gifts* of the Holy Spirit are wisdom, understanding, counsel, fortitude, knowledge, piety, and fear of the Lord....They complete and perfect the virtues (habitual and firm disposition to do good) of those who receive them.... (#1831)

Bible Verse

Isaiah 11:2

What You Will Learn

To identify the gifts of the Spirit: wisdom, understanding, counsel, fortitude, knowledge, piety, and awe (fear of the Lord)

To determine how these gifts are reflected in our lives

Supplies

Bible
Direction sheet
Markers or pencils in a variety of colors
Worksheet "The Gifts of the Spirit"
Gift box containing slips with the seven gifts of the Spirit

Directions for Center

- Read Isaiah 11:2.

- Read the information and directions.

- The candidate and parent/sponsor each choose one slip at a time from the gift box and on the sheet provided illustrate how they might use this specific gift. Continue until all the gifts have been selected. Return the slips to the box.

- Quietly say a prayer, thanking God for these gifts of the Spirit.

Background

Though these gifts were already received at baptism, we focus on them more fully with the celebration of confirmation. As we grow older we have a deeper understanding of them. The Spirit of God breathes upon us and deepens our wisdom, understanding, counsel, fortitude, knowledge, piety, and awe (fear of the Lord).

The Gifts of the Spirit

After selecting a slip from the gift box, illustrate in each box how can you demonstrate this gift.

WISDOM	UNDERSTANDING	COUNSEL
The ability to recognize our limitations and strengths and to deepen our experience of God	To keep open minds as we search for faith and truth wherever it leads	To make right judgments through reflection, prayer, and action, and to help others do the same

FORTITUDE	KNOWLEDGE	PIETY (LOVE)
To give courageous witness to our faith and to issues of peace and justice for all	To learn God's plan for us by using our gifts of spiritual insight	To recognize God as giver of all good gifts and to treat others and all creation with reverence

AWE (FEAR OF THE LORD)

To give glory and praise to the God of mystery and to acknowledge that all created things are gifts from God

You Receive Special "Fruits"

Goal

To demonstrate how the fruits of the Spirit are expressed in the choices we make
Through our attitudes and behaviors, we reveal the presence of the Spirit

Church Teaching

Catechism of the Catholic Church, paragraph 1832

The *fruits* of the Spirit are perfections that the Holy Spirit forms in us as the first fruits of eternal glory. The tradition of the church lists twelve of them: charity, joy, peace, patience, kindness, goodness, generosity, gentleness, faithfulness, modesty, self-control, chastity.

Bible Verse

Galatians 5:22–23

What You Will Learn

To identify the fruits of the Spirit as they are expressed in our lives
To find ways to consciously give witness to these fruits of the Spirit in our lives; when we practice them there can be no room for sin in our lives

Supplies
Bible
Direction sheet
Handout "Reflection on the Fruits of the Spirit"
Worksheet "The Fruits of the Spirit Blog"

Directions for Center

- Read Galatians 5:22–23.

- Read the information and directions.

- Talk about the dove as a symbol for the Holy Spirit, a way to express the beauty, peacefulness, and freedom of the Spirit in our lives.

- Discuss this quote with your parent/sponsor: "By your fruits you will know them."

- Use the worksheet "The Fruits of the Spirit Blog" to become a "blogger" and write your spontaneous feelings about one of the fruits of the Holy Spirit in your life or the lives of others around you.

Background

The fruits of the Holy Spirit express in reality the ways both early and present Christians were/are called to follow Jesus.

generosity   **SELF-CONTROL**

charity

FAITHFULNESS   *patience*

PEACE   JOY

goodness

modesty

CHASTITY   *gentleness*

Reflection on the Fruits of the Spirit

JOY: a feeling of happiness deep within you that comes from God

What is the difference between internal and external joy? Can you have joy even in the midst of sadness? What if your name were Joy? How would you live up to it?

LONG-SUFFERING: to patiently endure wrongs done to you, especially when they are unjust

How do you react when someone wrongs you? Do you ever ask God for guidance?

PATIENCE: to keep our balance when we are in a hurry or angry with the pace of others

Do you ever try to feel what others are feeling? Is waiting very difficult for you? Do you ask God to give you patience in difficult situations?

PEACE: to resolve conflicts without violence; an inner sense that God is with us and our world

How do you handle the conflicts in your daily life? Do you have an inner sense of God's presence?

KINDNESS: to treat all others with graciousness and goodwill; manners and etiquette are also in this mix; they show we have respect for others and look out for their good

How would you judge yourself on kindness?

GENEROSITY: to give as much as we can without expecting return; gratitude is one of the ways we respond to the blessings we have received

How do you express gratitude for your gifts and blessings? Do you give without expecting something in return?

SELF-CONTROL: to know our own limits and to exercise restraint as necessary; to have discipline is another way to describe self-control; the words "discipline" and "disciple" come from the same root word

How do you respond to the word "discipline"? Are there areas in your life that could use this virtue?

MODESTY: to be truthful about who we are, but not to brag or boast in order to make ourselves seem better and others less competent

Do you feel that you truly know yourself? How do you react to praise and/or criticism?

CHARITY: to love those we may not know personally as God loves them; the Latin word for "charity" is *caritas*, which is used in reference to God's love

Have you ever thought about loving those you don't personally know? In practical terms, how might you do this?

GOODNESS: to be aware of the needs of others and to choose to do the right thing

To be "good" sounds so simple. Do you consider yourself good? In what ways?

CHASTITY: to abstain from sexual intimacy until married and even when married to respect one another's sexuality

Have you given serious thought to this virtue? Do you ask God to strengthen you to practice it?

GENTLENESS: to respect self and others as children of God, to treat one another with care and concern

What comes to mind when you think of gentleness? In what ways do you offer care and concern to others?

Use this sheet to "blog" about one the fruits of the Holy Spirit. In what ways can you practice it? In what ways do others around you practice it?

The Fruits of the Spirit

About me

You Can Give Spiritual Gifts

Goal

To understand that the works of mercy are ways to be of service to our neighbors

Church Teaching

Catechism of the Catholic Church, paragraph 2447

The works of mercy are charitable actions by which we come to the aid of our neighbor in [his/her] spiritual and bodily necessities. Instructing, advising, consoling, comforting are spiritual works of mercy, as are forgiving and bearing wrongs patiently.

Bible Verse

Matthew 25:31–46

What You Will Learn

The spiritual works of mercy are: instructing the ignorant, admonishing the sinner, bearing wrongs patiently, forgiving injuries, counseling the doubtful, comforting the sorrowful, praying for the living and the dead

The works of mercy are both works of justice (long-term acts) and charity (immediate acts) pleasing to God

Supplies

Bible
Direction sheet
Handout "How to Practice the Spiritual Works of Mercy"
Worksheet "Texts of Mercy"
Pencils

Directions for Center

- Read Matthew 25:31–46.

- Read the information and directions.

- Read through the list and descriptions of the spiritual works of mercy.

- On the "Texts of Mercy" worksheet, write a message to someone you know indicating how you might be able to help them with a specific spiritual work of mercy.

Background

Service projects should not happen just because someone in the parish needs help or because students think they "have to" do a number of hours of service. The works of mercy have always been and will always be an important part of our gospel and Catholic/Christian tradition because they are the right thing to do.

How to Practice the Spiritual Works of Mercy

Which of these do you already do?

Instruct the ignorant
- ❏ help younger siblings or other children with homework
- ❏ tutor other students who need help with classes
- ❏ work with an ESL program
- ❏ help at a head start program
- ❏ help in a religious education program

Admonish the sinner
- ❏ talk to or pray for friends in trouble
- ❏ help them find professional help if they need it

Be patient with those who hurt you
- ❏ especially those whose actions you do not understand, with people who may be jealous of you

Forgive injuries
- ❏ give up old grudges
- ❏ forgive a friend who has offended you
- ❏ make family peace

Counsel the doubtful
- ❏ take time to listen to others
- ❏ reach out to those who seem alone or friendless

Comfort the sorrowing
- ❏ visit someone who has lost a loved one
- ❏ help someone who has lost a job
- ❏ visit someone in a nursing home
- ❏ help at a place like "Turning Points"
- ❏ work with immigrants or refugees

Pray for the living and the dead
- ❏ celebrate All Souls Day in November
- ❏ put the anniversaries of family/ friend members who have died on your family calendar
- ❏ each day, pray for a different member of your family
- ❏ take an older person to visit the cemetery where his/her loved ones are buried
- ❏ attend the funeral of a family friend with your parents

Texts of Mercy

Send a text message to a friend, family member, or acquaintance about the spiritual works of mercy and suggest ways you might practice them.

Counseling the doubtful

To:

Mary

Text:

I no ur worried bout spending 2 much time w/ ur boyfriend. Plz let me no if u want 2 talk about it.

Admonishing the sinner

To:

Text:

Bearing wrongs patiently

To:

Text:

Forgiving injuries

To:

Text:

Comforting the sorrowful

To:

Text:

Praying for the living and the dead

To:

Text:

Instructing the ignorant

To:

Text:

You Care for Others

Goal

To understand that the corporal works of mercy urge us to reach out with gospel service to people who are in need

Church Teaching

Catechism of the Catholic Church, paragraph 2447

The corporal works of mercy consist especially in feeding the hungry, sheltering the homeless, clothing the naked, visiting the sick and imprisoned, and burying the dead. Among all these, giving alms to the poor is one of the chief witnesses to fraternal charity: it is also a work of justice pleasing to God.

Bible Verse

Matthew 25:31–46

What You Will Learn

- The corporal works of mercy are: 1) feed the hungry; 2) visit the sick; 3) give drink to the thirsty; 4) clothe the naked; 5) shelter the homeless; 6) bury the dead; 7) visit the imprisoned
- It is not always easy to do the work of the gospel; the social gospel means reaching out to those in need without judging them
- To distinguish between justice and charity—both are necessary for true change to occur

Supplies

Bible
Direction sheet
Handout "How to Practice Corporal Works of Mercy"
Booklet "Certificates for the Corporal Works of Mercy"
Pencils/markers

Direction for Center

- Read Matthew 25:31–46.

- Read the information and directions.

- Take one of the booklets of certificates:
  1) select people whom you can serve in one of these ways;
  2) if it is appropriate, give the certificates to the people you have selected.

Background

Service projects are not about doing "x" number of hours of service. The works of mercy speak to us of what it means to be a Christian, the body of Christ. We are the members, and Christ the head. Together we reach out to all in need—even when it makes demands on us.

How to Practice
Corporal Works of Mercy

Which of these do you already do?

Feed the hungry
- ❏ work at a food shelter
- ❏ donate to a "Feed the Hungry" project

Visit the sick
- ❏ work at a hospital as a volunteer;
- ❏ visit a friend who is ill

Give drink to the thirsty
- ❏ conserve water
- ❏ do not use plastic water bottles
- ❏ give workers a cool drink of water

Clothe the naked
- ❏ give good used clothing to Good Will
- ❏ do not buy "brand" clothes that may be more expensive
- ❏ when you buy something new give something old away

Shelter the homeless
- ❏ donate a blanket for the homeless
- ❏ work at a homeless shelter
- ❏ tutor homeless children

Bury the dead
- ❏ send a card to someone who has recently lost a parent or other family member

Visit the imprisoned
- ❏ think and pray for people who find themselves "locked up" in either body or spirit

Certificates for the
Corporal Works of Mercy

Visit the Imprisoned

To: My Grandmother
I will: Come to the nursing home to visit you each month
From: Your grandson, Tom

Feed the Hungry

To: _____
I will: _____
From: _____

Visit the Sick

To: _____
I will: _____
From: _____

Give Drink to the Thirsty

To: _____

I will: _____

From: _____

Clothe the Naked

To: _____

I will: _____

From: _____

Shelter the Homeless

To: _____

I will: _____

From: _____

Bury the Dead

To: _____

I will: _____

From: _____

You Stand Up
for Others
(Catholic Social Teachings)

Goal

To learn that the sacrament of confirmation is part of our initiation into the church, and with this initiation we take upon ourselves the promise to enact the Catholic Church's social teachings/principles

Church Teachings

Catechism of the Catholic Church, paragraph 2422

The Church's social teaching comprises a body of doctrine which is articulated as the Church interprets events in the course of history, with the assistance of the Holy Spirit, in the light of the whole of what has been revealed by Jesus Christ. This teaching can be more easily accepted by men of good will, the more the faithful let themselves be guided by it.

Bible Verse

Matthew 6:24
Luke 16:13, 19–32

What You Will Learn

To know the social teachings of the church as part of Christian revelation and tradition: 1) dignity of the human person; 2) community and the common good; 3) people's rights and responsibilities; 4) option for the poor and vulnerable; 5) solidarity and global justice; 6) care for God's creation; 7) dignity of work and rights of workers

To consider how to live these out in local and global ways

To name places and pray for the people in the world where these may not be observed

Supplies

Bible

Direction sheet

Handout "Ways to Live Out Catholic Social Teachings"

Slips of paper "Social Teaching Review Dates"

Envelopes for the slips with the dates written on outside

Pencils, scissors

Magazines/newspapers

Directions for Center

- Read Matthew 6:24 and Luke 16:13, 19–32.

- Read the information and directions.

- Read through the goals for the various social teachings with suggestions for living them out; discuss these with your parent/sponsor.

- Take a magazine or newspaper and find articles that refer to one of these teachings.

- On the boxes provided on the worksheet, fill in the way you will try to observe this social teaching as part of your life. Put these in an envelope for later reference on the church feast days suggested below.

   March 25: Annunciation (Incarnation) (Dignity of the Human Person)

   April: Holy Week and Easter Sunday (Community and Common Good)

   May 1: St. Joseph the Worker (Dignity of Work and the Rights of Workers)

   September 14: Holy Cross (Solidarity and Global Justice)

   October 4: St. Francis of Assisi (Care for God's Creation)

   November: Thanksgiving (People's Rights and Responsibilities)

   December 25: Christmas (Option for the Poor and Vulnerable)

Background

Throughout the last 125 years the popes have written encyclicals/letters calling on Christians to respond to these social principles. *The Document on the Church in the Modern World* from Vatican II may be the clearest statement on this role of the living active church today.

Ways to Live Out
Catholic Social Teachings

Dignity of the Human Person
This calls not only for the protection of unborn and newborn life, but of all life. Every person has dignity and deserves respect by virtue of being created in God's image.

Community and the Common Good
It is natural for people to be involved in communities. This is where people grow as individuals and together work for the common good of all. The needs of all the members of the community should be met. This includes our national and world communities.

Solidarity and Global Justice
As children of one God, all peoples of the world are members of one family; solidarity means we are all related to, and responsible for, one another. We live in a global family.

Option for the Poor and Vulnerable
We are called to have special concern for those who have special needs of body and spirit: the handicapped, children, widows, homeless, immigrants, aged, the sick, etc. We address these needs with both charity and justice. Justice changes systems; charity takes care of immediate needs.

Dignity of Work and the Rights of Workers
Through work we participate in God's creativity and serve others. Work has dignity and it benefits others. All workers have rights but they also have responsibilities.

People's Rights and Responsibilities
All people have basic rights and responsibilities that are to be respected. Our government refers to these as life, liberty, and the pursuit of happiness. People who do not live in democratic societies still have the same basic rights.

Care for God's Creation
This shows the respect we have for God, our Creator. The goods of the earth are gifts from God and are to benefit all people, God's gifts are not be misused or hoarded for personal gain. Care of the earth is a moral duty.

Social Teaching Review Dates

Fill out these slips for future reference.

On the feast day of **MARCH 25, THE ANNUNCIATION,** I will review how I have been concerned about *the dignity of the human person* in the following way…

In **APRIL, DURING HOLY WEEK AND EASTER,** I will review how I have been concerned about *the community and the common good* in the following way…

On the feast day of **MAY 1, ST. JOSEPH THE WORKER,** I will review how I have been concerned about *the dignity of work and the rights of workers* in the following way…

On the feast day of **SEPTEMBER 14, HOLY CROSS,** I will review how I have been concerned about *solidarity and global justice* in the following way…

On the feast day of **OCTOBER 4, ST. FRANCIS OF ASSISI**, I will review how I have been concerned about *the care for God's creation* in the following way…

In **NOVEMBER, ON THANKSGIVING**, I will review how I have been concerned about *people's rights and responsibilities* in the following way…

On **DECEMBER 25, CHRISTMAS**, I will review how I have been concerned about *the option for the poor and vulnerable* in the following way…

Your Choices Make a Difference

Goal

To recognize that serious sin is the source of unhappiness and pain. Choices we make have long-term effects. Since "two things cannot be in the same place at the same time," fruits of the Spirit and sins cannot exist together

Church Teaching

Catechism of the Catholic Church, paragraph 1866

Vices can be classified according to the virtues they oppose, or also be linked to the capital sins….They are called "capital" because they engender other sins, other vices. They are pride, avarice, envy, wrath, lust, gluttony, and sloth or acedia.

Bible Verse

2 Peter 1:3

What You Will Learn

We are all tempted to allow sin into our lives. The source of this is "original sin"

As faith-filled Christians, we focus on avoiding and defeating sin in our lives and replacing it with virtue

To admit that these sins "grow" and can become a "slippery slope" leading to greater vices in our personal lives

The gifts and fruits of the Spirit lead us to virtues rather than to vices

Purity of heart dismisses sin and embraces what is good (virtues)

Supplies
Bible
Direction sheet
Worksheet "Activity One"
Worksheet "Activity Two"

Directions for Center

- Read 2 Peter 1:3.

- Read the information and directions.

- *Activity One:* Think about the movies, music, and TV programs that you choose to watch or listen to. How do these either glorify sin or show that it is destructive? Follow the directions on the sheet provided for your ideas.

- *Activity Two:* Think about how one sin can lead to greater sin in the future.

Background

Some sins are traditionally listed by the church as capital or deadly because they are so serious. Sin is the enemy of happiness and starts in the mind. The capital sins (also known as the seven deadly sins) are pride, avarice (greed), envy, anger, lust, gluttony, and sloth (acedia). "Capital" means having the greatest influence. When we remove these sins from our lives, we can make room for grace to enter.

The seven deadly sins versus the fruits of the Spirit

lust	modesty and chastity
greed	charity and generosity
anger	patience and joy
sloth (laziness in our life of faith)	peace and goodness
jealousy	gentleness and kindness
pride	long-suffering
gluttony	self-control

Making Good and Moral Choices
Activity One

The "capital-deadly" sins are often used as themes in movies, songs, or TV shows. Below write the names of movies, songs, or TV shows beside each sin and place a plus sign (+) or minus sign (-) if it does or does not reflect your beliefs and values.

	MOVIE	SONG	TV SHOW
Greed / Avarice			
Pride / Vanity			
Envy / Jealousy			
Lust / Uncontrolled Desires			
Gluttony			
Sloth / Acedia			
Anger			

Making Good and Moral Choices

Activity Two

Choices you make or actions you do today can sometimes lead to vice or virtue in your life, happiness or unhappiness. How might what you do today lead to greater sin in your future?

Greed/Avarice *(always wanting more)*

Today...	In two weeks...	How might you overcome this vice today?

Pride/Vanity *(considering yourself the best)*

Today...	In two weeks...	How might you overcome this vice today?

Envy/Jealousy *(wanting what others have)*

Today...	In two weeks...	How might you overcome this vice today?

Lust (*uncontrolled desires*)

Today...	In two weeks...	How might you overcome this vice today?

Gluttony (*seeking too much of any good thing*)

Today...	In two weeks...	How might you overcome this vice today?

Sloth/Acedia (*laziness in spiritual life*)

Today...	In two weeks...	How might you overcome this vice today?

Anger (*strong feelings of annoyance or hostility*)

Today...	In two weeks...	How might you overcome this vice today?

The Church Gives You Rules

Goal

To realize that any organization to which we belong has rules for the sake of order As full members of the church we are expected to keep its precepts or laws

Church Teaching

Catechism of the Catholic Church, paragraphs 2041–2043

The precepts of the church are set in the context of moral life bound to and nourished by liturgical life. The obligatory character of these positive laws decreed by the pastoral authorities is meant to guarantee to the faithful the very necessary minimum in the spirit of prayer and moral effort, in the growth of love of God and neighbor.

Bible Verse

Ephesians 4:11–20

What You Will Learn

These are the precepts or laws of the church:
» Attend Mass on Sundays and holy days and rest from unnecessary work
» Confess your sins at least once a year
» Receive the sacrament of Eucharist at least during the Easter season
» Observe the days of fasting and abstinence as directed by the church
» Help to provide for the needs, financial and otherwise, of the church

These precepts are only minimal directions; in living a moral Christian life, sacraments are the primary way to experience Christ's presence at important times in our lives

Supplies

Bible
Direction sheet
Worksheet "Reflecting Spiritually on Church Laws"

Directions for Center

- Read Ephesians 4:11–20.

- Read the information and directions.

- Often it is difficult for young people to see the need or value of keeping the precepts/laws of the church. What reasons might young people today give for NOT keeping them? What reasons would you give for keeping them? Fill in the spaces on the chart.

Background

Church precepts are made by church authority (canon law). Jesus told us that it is not only laws, but the Spirit that gives life. These precepts give us the very minimum we need, in the spirit of prayer, to grow in love of God and neighbor. These precepts are nourished by and given life through the liturgical life of the church. We acknowledge they are important to our membership in the church.

Reflecting Spiritually on Church Laws

	Attend Mass on Sundays	Confess sins (reconciliation at least once a year)	Receive the Eucharist during the Easter season	Fasting as directed during Lent	Contributions (time, talent, treasure for the needs of the church)
Why would you keep this precept?					
Excuses young people use to neglect it					
How would you respond to these excuses?					

Your Life in the Spirit
(Mystagogia)

Goal
To understand that mystagogy (the mystery of Christ) is the last of the stages of the RCIA (Rite of Christian Initiation) but it lasts an entire lifetime

Church Teaching
Catechism of the Catholic Church, paragraph 1075

Catechesis aims to initiate people into the mystery of Christ (it is "mystagogy") by proceeding from the visible to the invisible, from the sign to the thing signified, from the "sacraments" to the "mysteries."

Bible Verse
Ephesians 6:18–20

What You Will Learn
To understand that mystagogia involves a lifetime of involvement in the church and growing in one's faith through study, prayer, and action

To carry out the responsibility of the covenant you have made with God—to be an active member of the Christian community

To acknowledge confirmation as a beginning of your faith journey

To embrace the paschal mystery as the core of your faith life

Supplies

Bible
Direction sheet
Worksheet "Journal Page"
Pencils
Envelopes for each student

Directions for Center

- Read Ephesians 6:18–20.

- Read the information and directions.

- Take a journal page.

  a. Write a prayer thanking the Spirit of God, who is, has been, and will be with you in your life. This prayer can be your covenant, your promise to be faithful to the initiation process for which you have been preparing since baptism. Keep this covenant in a file with your important papers. About every six months, take it out, read it, and see if you have been faithful to your part of the covenant with God.

  b. Answer the three questions on your journal page(s).

- Pray the closing prayer with your parent/sponsor.

Background

When the rites of initiation are completed, those baptized and confirmed and partaking of the Eucharist are asked to continue their catechesis and experience the mysteries of Christ in their lives. They continue to spend time in study and action as a Christian. This presumes that once young people have been confirmed, the study of their faith and what it means will not be the end of their formal study. They will now become lifelong learners of their faith and religion.

COMMITMENT PRAYER SERVICE

Parent/Sponsor *Read* Acts of Apostles 8:14–22, 25

Candidate I, (*name*), with the support
of my family, my sponsor, and this parish,
commit myself to complete my sacramental initiation
by preparing to receive the sacrament of confirmation.
I understand that by committing myself to this process,
I accept the responsibility to learn more about my faith,
to serve others willingly,
to reflect on and deepen my relationship with the Holy Spirit,
and to become a witness of gospel values
and the moral teachings of the church.

Parent/Sponsor (*Lay your hands on the shoulder of the candidate and pray silently for him/her for a few minutes*)

Offer one another a sign of peace.

Journal Page

Prayer of thanksgiving to the Spirit of God:

1. How will you continue to live your faith?

2. How will you continue to learn more about your faith in the years to come?

3. How might you hand on your faith if you are someday blessed with children?